EXPLORING

Inner Cities

Danielle Sensier and
Amanda Earl

WAYLAND

Landmarks

Exploring Inner Cities

Exploring Seaside Towns

Exploring Suburbs

Exploring Villages

Cover: Bristol City Centre (main picture); the Docklands light railway (top); and Notting Hill Carnival (bottom left).
Title page: Birmingham's inner-city skyline.
Contents page: A young girl enjoys the fun of Notting Hill Carnival, in London.

For the Writeaway Group, and in memory of Jenny Stoker.

Series editor: Katie Orchard
Designer: Tim Mayer/Mark Whitchurch
Production controller: Carol Stevens
Artist: Clive Spong (Linden Artists)

First published in 1997 by Wayland Publishers Limited
61 Western Road, Hove
East Sussex, BN3 1JD, England

© Copyright 1997 Wayland Publishers Limited

British Library Cataloguing in Publication Data
Sensier, Danielle
    Exploring Inner Cities. – (Landmarks)
    1. Inner cities – juvenile literature
    I. Title II. Earl, Amanda
    307.7'6

ISBN 0 7502 1881 9

Typeset by Mayer Media/Mark Whitchurch Art & Design
Printed and bound in Italy by G. Canale S.p.A.

Picture acknowledgements:
Action Images 34 (bottom); Brindleyplace Plc 39, 43; Castlefield Urban Heritage Park 35, 42; James Davis Travel Photography **cover** (main picture), 5; Eye Ubiquitous/Tim Page **cover** (bottom left); Glasgow Development Agency 19 (both); Harland and Woolf Shipyards 15; Rupert Horrocks 11 (right); Impact photos Peter Arkell 12 (top)/John Arthur 12 (bottom)/ Martin Black 7/ Mike McQueen **cover** (top); Guy Moberly **contents page**/ Colin Shaw **title page**, 10 / Simon Shepheard 4 (both), 6 (bottom), 8, 17 (bottom), 18 (bottom), 20 (both), 22–23 (all), 24, 25 (bottom), 26, 27, 29 (top), 30, 31 (bottom), 34 (top), 36, 37, 40, 41 (both)/ Bruce Stephens 6 (top), 11 (top), 13, 14 (top), 18 (top), 28, 31 (top)/ Geray Sweeney 16/ Stewart Weir 9 (top); Manchester City Council, Marketing © 38; Ordnance Survey 21; Stephen White-Thomson 11 (bottom). Map on page 47 is by Peter Bull and artwork on pages 33–34 is by Clive Spong.

Contents

What is an Inner City?

An inner city is a large, built-up area which has grown up around a city centre. Inner cities are densely populated areas. They are busy, noisy places, full of people, cars and traffic. Inner cities are called urban settlements.

SETTLEMENT	POPULATION
City	Over 100,000
Town	2,000–100,000
Village	100–2,000

More than half of the people in the UK live in a town or city. The rest of the population either live in suburbs on the edges of towns and cities, or in villages.

Some cities are very large. London is the largest city in the UK. Nearly 7 million people live there, and walking from the centre to its boundary could take you all day!

Above Urban settlements are very busy places. This picture was taken in Leeds.

Left Liverpool's Liver Building is a famous landmark. It stands beside the River Mersey, whose docks once brought great wealth to the city.

Inner cities have many different types of buildings, such as houses, tower blocks, factories and shops. These buildings have developed over hundreds of years, so cities usually have a mixture of old and new buildings. Cities are also important centres for medicine and learning. You will usually find large hospitals and universities there.

Inner cities have a great variety of old and new buildings. In this picture of Bristol, you can see local shops, a multi-storey car park, high-rise flats, modern offices and, in the distance, an old church.

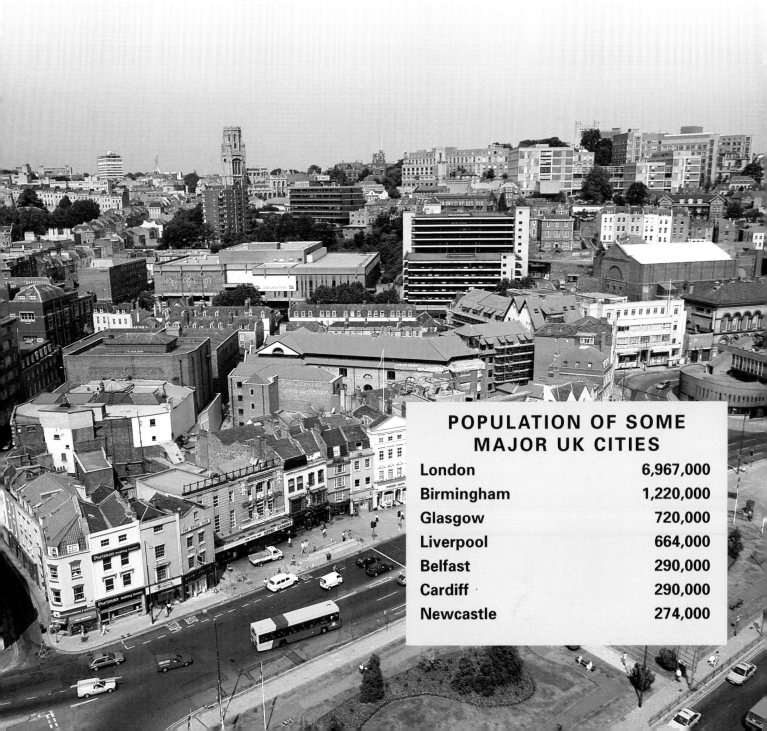

POPULATION OF SOME MAJOR UK CITIES	
London	6,967,000
Birmingham	1,220,000
Glasgow	720,000
Liverpool	664,000
Belfast	290,000
Cardiff	290,000
Newcastle	274,000

There are several reasons why many industrial cities grew up where they did. Being close to a river estuary led to the development of thriving ports. Natural resources, such as coal or iron ore made some areas ideal places for mines and factories. Cities grew even more with improved transport and communication, such as canals, bridges, roads and railways. If you look around an inner city, you will see the evidence of these natural and artificial features all around you.

Above These ultra-modern office blocks tower over Birmingham's Gas Street Canal.

In today's inner cities, the canal networks are used for leisure rather than industry. Here, in Manchester, you can see people enjoying a walk along the tow path.

A view across London. High rise buildings surround the central business district. The outskirts of London are less built up.

How cities develop

If you look at a city plan, you can see how the city has developed. Most cities follow a similar pattern. At the centre is the central business district (CBD), surrounded by the inner city. On the edges of the inner city are the suburbs and beyond this, in the countryside, you will find villages.

Activity

Inner cities have developed around the central business district (CBD) – the area where a city first began. Here, there are important buildings, such as the civic centre, law courts, museums and theatres. The CBD is also the main commercial centre, with large banks, department stores and offices. Find a city plan in a road atlas, and locate some of these buildings. This will help you to find the CBD.

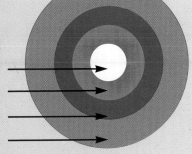

Central Business District
Inner City
Suburbs
Villages

People and Communities

When you look around an inner city, one of the first things you will notice is the number of people living there. An inner city has a large population made up of different groups of people. These groups live in communities called neighbourhoods. The houses and buildings are built very close together. With so many people in one area, the buildings all jostle together for space.

Who lives in an inner city?

Cities have always attracted people moving from other settlements in search of jobs. During the Industrial Revolution, many people moved from the countryside to towns to look for work in the new factories. As more people arrived, new houses and buildings sprang up everywhere. Industrial centres such as Manchester, Liverpool and Glasgow grew into great cities. Today, inner cities are home to a variety of people, many of whose ancestors once worked in the early factories.

Inner cities are full of people. At this market in Leeds, everyone is busy doing their shopping.

Jenny Stoker, Newcastle-Upon-Tyne

Seventy-nine-year-old, Jenny Stoker from Newcastle-upon-Tyne, belongs to a writers' group called Writeaway. The members of the group sometimes write down their memories of the past and the changes they have seen.

'In the 1920s when I was a child, we had no hot water and no baths. The men who did have work were mainly miners, shipyard workers or factory workers, so not having hot water was very unfair,' remembers Jenny.

The first improvement in Newcastle that Jenny remembers was the building of pit head baths. This meant that the miners could go home clean instead of having to use a tin bath in front of the fire.

Jenny continues: *'Then the council started knocking down the old buildings and replacing them with new flats, which had modern kitchens and bathrooms. People started to become interested in improving their surroundings.'*

Above The Tyne Bridge in Newcastle a famous landmark, built when the city was a great industrial centre.

Left Jenny Stoker. Elderly people are a very important source of information about an area. They have often seen many of the changes for themselves.

9

Below In inner cities, large, religious buildings, such as mosques and cathedrals are a feature of the city skyline, alongside flats and offices.

In the 1950s and 1960s, inner cities once again attracted people who were encouraged to work there. This time, the newcomers came from other parts of the world, such as the West Indies, India, Pakistan and Bangladesh. More recently, there have been refugees from other countries, such as Vietnam, Bosnia and Kurdistan. All these different ethnic groups bring a variety of languages, food, clothes and religions. In London, more than 60,000 Muslims worship at the Central Mosque, and in Leicester, during the Hindu festival of Diwali, the streets are filled with thousands of colourful lights and there are special fireworks.

Above Terraced houses, 1960s tower blocks and low-rise flats are some of the types of housing found in inner-cities.

Inner-city homes

Most inner cities have a mixture of old and new buildings. You can often see rows of terraced houses, once built for factory workers and their families. Huge, concrete tower blocks, each containing hundreds of flats, also stand out along city skylines. In the 1960s, many terraced houses were knocked down to make way for tower blocks, which provided many homes on a small area of land. This was popular with town planners, but less so with the people who moved into them. Today, modern inner-city homes are built in small groups with gardens, as it has been found that this is what most people prefer.

Activity

The number of people living in an area is recorded in a census, which is carried out every ten years. The last one was in 1991. Here are some of the results from Glasgow:

Age group	Number of children
0–4	42,967
5–9	40,790
10–14	37,629

Finding out how many children live in an area helps planners to decide how many schools will be needed in the future. Use census information from your local library to find out how many children aged 0–14 live in your area.

Small gardens allow people to get away from the noise and bustle of the inner city.

Work and play

Work in inner cities is not the same as it used to be. There are fewer jobs because many shops and factories have closed down. People still come to big cities to look for work, but many are unsuccessful and become unemployed. Without jobs, some people even become homeless.

Right These homeless people have found some shelter in a shop doorway.

Below There is always something to do in an inner city. These children are taking part in London's Notting Hill Carnival.

For most people, however, inner cities are busy and exciting places to live, where there are lots of things happening. People need services such as shops, schools and places for entertainment and worship. Inner-city communities have a great variety of these facilities, providing people with more choice than they would have in a village or suburb.

Children in inner cities often have some of the most modern sports facilities in the UK. These boys are playing football on astro-turf.

Even so, some inner-city areas are no longer attractive places to live in because of problems such as derelict buildings, pollution and fear of crime. This has encouraged many people to move out of inner cities to suburbs and villages in search of a better environment.

GLASGOW'S INDUSTRIAL GROWTH

Year	Population	Patterns of change
1791	66,000	Glasgow's population grows during Industrial Revolution
1891	658,073	Industrial production is at its peak – the main jobs are in the steel and shipbuilding industries
1939	1,128,473	Highest population
1994	680,000	14% of jobs are in manufacturing – light engineering, clothing, food and drink and publishing. 80% of jobs are in the service industry – Glasgow is the second-largest region for services in the UK.

Earning a Living

Above In inner cities today, most jobs are in the service industries. Clothes stores provide many of these jobs.

The busiest part of a settlement is a good place to start finding out about jobs. In an inner city, this is often at a local shopping parade. Here you will find people working in shops and offices, such as food stores, small banks and take-away restaurants. They provide goods and services for their customers, who might be buying groceries, getting money from the bank, or just ordering a pizza!

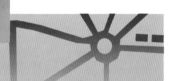

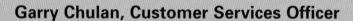

CASE STUDY

Garry Chulan, Customer Services Officer

Garry Chulan is a Customer Services Officer with the NatWest Bank. Garry's bank is at one of their largest branches in the city centre of Nottingham.

Everything inside the bank is very modern, but the building is over 100 years old. It's in the centre of Nottingham, close to the town hall, the market square and all the big shops and offices.

The street outside is always busy, but cars are only allowed to use it at certain times of the day. Garry gets into work by bus. It's much easier and he doesn't have to worry about parking.

'I meet lots of people in my job. Sometimes we have as many as 250 customers a day,' says Garry.

Above Garry Chulan at his desk.

The jobs found at a local shopping parade are part of the service industry, which also includes people working in hospitals, schools and office headquarters in the city centre. Service jobs are the main type of employment in an inner-city area.

Inner cities have fewer manufacturing jobs now than they did in the past. This is because goods such as cars, clothes and washing machines can

DECLINE IN MANUFACTURING JOBS

| 1955 | 42% of UK workforce in manufacturing |
| 1996 | 21% of UK workforce in manufacturing |

now be made more cheaply in other countries. Industries such as coal mining, steel manufacturing and shipbuilding, which once created so many jobs, have now declined.

Left The docklands areas of the UK used to be part of a thriving industry, which provided thousands of jobs. Today, docks such as the Harland and Woolf shipyard in Belfast are either closed down or are only just surviving, building just a few ships a year.

Inner cities would have been very different during the early 1900s, when millions of inner-city workers were employed in factories, shipyards and mines. At this time, around 60 per cent of all the world's ships were made in the UK. Luxury ocean liners, such as the *Titanic* were built in Belfast, and cutlery made from Sheffield Steel was used all over the world. Manchester was so successful at making cloth, that the city became known as King Cotton!

WORKING POPULATION IN THE UK

Service Industry	72%
Manufacturing	21%
Construction	4%
Others	3%

You can still see the famous Linen Hall in Linen Hall Street, Belfast. It is an important clue to industry in the past. Belfast was once known as the 'linen capital of the world', because it exported tonnes of fine Irish linen cloth.

Max Butler, Staff Nurse

Max Butler lives in Lenton, in Nottingham. She works as a staff nurse at the Queens Medical Centre there. It's a big hospital in the inner city. Max is a shift worker, which means that she often has to work through the night and sleep during the day.

'Queen's Medical Centre is a huge hospital, with more than 41 km of corridor!' says Max.

Left Max Butler.

Evidence of these thriving industries can still be found in the names of inner-city areas and buildings. The name of the Jewellery Quarter in Birmingham provides a useful clue about the jobs that people used to have there. The Picton Library in Liverpool was named after Sir James Allanson Picton, who ran a large printing works in the city during the nineteenth century.

Right Albert Docks in Liverpool has found a new lease of life as many of its old warehouse buildings have been turned into cafés, restaurants, and workshops.

17

Unemployment

Today, more than 2.5 million people in the UK are unable to find work. Unemployment is particularly high in inner-city areas, where there is little industry but a large population. For example, in Liverpool, in 1985, around 12 per cent of the working-age population were unemployed.

Above In many cities, modern industries are beginning to provide new jobs, which help reduce unemployment. This factory in Cardiff makes microwave ovens.

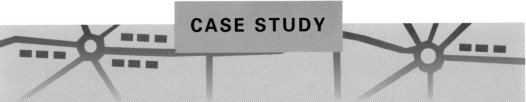

CASE STUDY

Water Court Job Centre, Nottingham

In May 1996, about 32,670 people in Nottingham were unemployed – that's nearly 10 per cent. A job centre is one of the places where unemployed people can get help to find a job. Water Court Job Centre is in a renovated warehouse near the centre of Nottingham.

There are ninety staff at Water Court Job Centre. They try to match job seekers with employers. Details of new jobs are displayed on cards, showing the amount of pay and hours for each job. There isn't much manufacturing work in the local area and many of the jobs are part time.

Left Water Court job centre.

Activity

Try using a questionnaire to get an idea of the different types of jobs where you live. Ask your parents, grandparents and neighbours, and get your friends to do the same. Record the answers on a chart, or if you have access to a computer use a database. The results could look something like this:

Questions	Frank	June	Adil
age now	65	48	27
age started work	14	17	21
job	retired steel worker	sales supervisor	surveyor
industry	manufacturing	service	construction

To create more jobs, some industries and new companies are now being encouraged to move to the inner cities. Special projects, such as the 'City Pride Initiatives', allow such companies or industries to buy land more cheaply and give them extra help with planning their new businesses. Derelict factories and warehouses are also being renovated to make space for new offices, shops and restaurants. This provides more jobs within the construction industry.

Before and after: Glasgow's Development Agency have helped to transform this run down industrial area of the city, providing new factories and improving the environment with green spaces and flowers.

Inner-City Schools

What is it like to go to an inner-city school? Actually, it is not very different from going to school in other types of settlement. In most places in the UK, the school day is very much the same: morning register, lessons, lunch and play. Whether you live in a village, suburb or city, you will probably recognize this pattern.

What is different about inner-city schools is the number of them. Cities have huge populations – including lots of children! Over the years, as cities have grown, more and more schools have been built. In Glasgow, there are 250 schools in an area of 202 km².

Above This inner-city school in London is part of a large housing estate. There is lots of concrete and tarmac, but there are plenty of trees, and new play equipment has been added.

Above Some inner-city schools have their own conservation areas, which attract birds, butterflies and insects.

There are more open spaces in an inner-city neighbourhood than you might think. On an inner-city map you might see parks, recreation grounds, allotments or football pitches. Even a derelict area can quickly become home to beautiful wild flowers and butterflies.

If you look around your school, you will start to get a picture of your local area. Inner-city schools are located in built-up areas, so from the window you would probably see houses, roads and shops, but not open fields. Inner cities have a wide variety of schools, which can be old, new, large or small.

Woodlands Park Junior School, in Tottenham, North London, has 220 pupils. It was built almost 100 years ago, and is a typical red-brick Victorian building. The Ordnance Survey map (right) shows the position of Woodlands Park School. On the map you can see houses, open spaces, roads as well as other interesting features, such as bus shelters and a church.

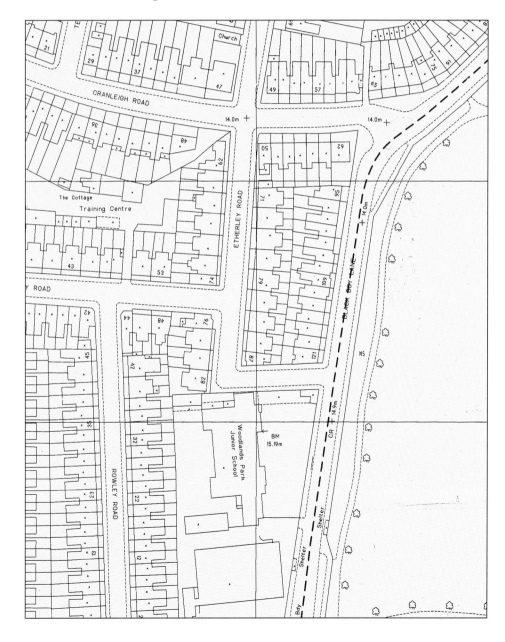

Woodlands Park Junior School and its surrounding area.

School features

When you take a closer look at an inner-city school, you may be able to find some interesting features. In many Victorian schools, the playgrounds have hard surfaces and there is no grass. In some of these buildings you can still see the words 'Girls' and 'Boys' above the doorways. When the schools were built, the girls and boys had to play in separate playgrounds and enter the school through different entrances. Many of these Victorian buildings are tall, with high ceilings and large windows. Some even have their own bell towers. They were built with popular materials of the time, such as red bricks, slate roof tiles and fancy iron railings.

What's in a name?

The name of a school is often linked with its surrounding area. Some schools are named after well-known local features or buildings, such as Mill Street School. Others are named after their local area, such as Queen's Park School. The names of the school founder, a famous person or saint are also used, such as Rudyard Kipling, or St Paul.

Right During the Second World War, many iron railings were taken away to be melted down and made into weapons. Luckily, these have survived!

Right The windows of Netley Street School are very tall, with fancy brickwork for decoration.

Above Does your school have a sign like this one? In Victorian times, these signs were very common because boys and girls had separate playgrounds.

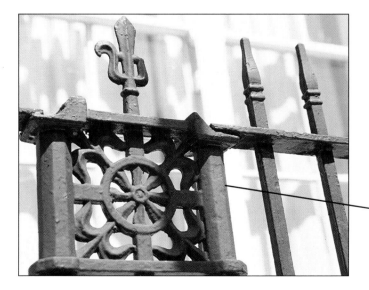

Netley Street School, in London, was built in Victorian times. It still has many old-fashioned features which give us clues about the area's past.

Your school environment

In some inner-city areas, old, Victorian schools have been knocked down and replaced with newer buildings. These are often single-storey buildings, built using modern materials, such as concrete and plastic, as well as brick. They may also have trees, grass and better areas for playing, such as adventure trails and playing fields.

Today, inner-city schools are working very hard to improve their environment. The children at St Benedict's School, in Coventry, have transformed their tarmac playground by designing their own stencils and painting them on the ground and walls. They have also created a wind chime garden and planted herbs and special plants to attract butterflies. Other schools with tarmac playgrounds have 'mini-gardens', where they can grow their own vegetables in grow bags.

Activity

Drawing a map of your school and the surrounding area will help you to investigate your local area. Draw a map of your school, showing the useful facilities around it, such as shops, parks, churches, bus stops, telephone boxes and post boxes. You could also include your own special landmarks, such as the sweet shop, a friend's house, or even the local friendly cat!

These flower designs really cheer up what used to be a dull brick wall at St Benedict's School, Coventry.

Woodroyd School's Tropical Rain Forest Mural

Joanne, Abid and Ali start work on their mural.

The children of Woodroyd Middle School in Bradford have transformed their inner-city playground. Instead of plain walls, three sides of the playground are now covered with a tropical rain forest mural.

The pupils, with the help of their art teacher, Shirley Elliot, first designed their mural inside, on large display boards. Then, they transferred their ideas to the playground walls.

The mural took two months to complete and each pupil has signed their own creature. Some have even painted their animals in the style of famous artists, such as Picasso and Van Gogh!

The project has encouraged the children to talk about the rain forests and the people who live there. It has also made their playground a bright and cheerful place to play.

Two months later, the mural is almost finished.

25

On the Move

Good transport and communication networks are very important in inner cities. Many thousands of people need to move around quickly and easily for work, or when they go shopping or go out in the evening. If you look around an inner city, you will see many types of transport, from trains and buses, to taxis, trams and cars. Some inner cities, such as London and Newcastle, have found that one of the most effective ways for people to get around is on the Underground. This is a network of trains, which runs through long, criss-crossing tunnels underneath the pavement.

St Pancras Station was built in 1868, and took six years to complete. Huge stations like this helped to improve communication links between cities.

Growing cities

All of the major cities in the UK have grown up with the help of good transport networks. Cities often developed near rivers, because goods could be transported easily from one place to another by boat. Ports and docks developed where cities where close to the sea.

London developed as a port around the River Thames, with many busy docks, such as the East India Docks. Such docks imported and exported goods all over the world. The East India Docks have now closed. But some of the docks, such as St Catherine's Dock in the heart of the city, have had a new lease of life. Many of the old docks are now used for leisure, with restaurants, cafés and pubs.

In an inner city there are many ways to get to school. This girl in London is using the Underground.

27

Canal barges used to carry many things, even hay, needed for the horse-drawn carriages used about 200 years ago. Now they often carry holiday-makers.

In inner cities such as Birmingham and Manchester, canals are an important feature. Canals were built over 200 years ago, and were a vital part of the cities' development. In the past, barges carried raw materials on the canals to the new factories and mills, and manufactured goods back to the big cities. In many inner cities today, you will still see these canal networks with their locks and bridges, but the barges are now used mainly by holiday-makers. During Victorian times, a vast network of railways was constructed in places where canals could not be built. The trains were much faster than the canal barges.

Sheffield's Supertram

Some cities have improved their transport networks by introducing modern trams. Sheffield's Supertram runs on track powered by electricity from overhead wires.

The Supertram is clean and kind to the environment. Unlike cars, it is quiet and does not give out any fumes. Each tramstop has ramps on the platform. The ramps make it easier for parents with pushchairs and people in wheelchairs to get on.

Nina Wybrant drives a Supertram with the help of a computer, which can even change the traffic lights to let the tram through.

Above One tram can carry as many as 250 passengers. Just think of how many cars that many people would use!

Right Nina Wybrant, a Supertram driver in Sheffield.

From the 1920s–1950s, more and more railways were built, connecting inner cities with other types of settlements such as suburbs and villages. For the first time, people were able to live in one place and work in another. Many people moved to the suburbs, but commuted to work in the city.

The environment

Today, as more people drive cars, inner cities are often very congested with traffic. This discourages new businesses from starting up in inner cities, because making deliveries, or just getting to work can take hours if you get caught in traffic. Inner-city planners know that one of their most important jobs is to improve the road and motorway networks in and around the inner cities.

Around 87 per cent of passenger journeys made in the UK are by car, taxi or motorbike.

Cycling is a very good way of getting around an inner city and beating the traffic! This cyclist is wearing a special mask to protect him from the car fumes. With fewer cars and more cyclists like this one, there would be a lot less pollution.

Public transport is being improved in the hope that it will help cut down on the number of cars being used, and reduce pollution. Buses can now travel more quickly in traffic-free bus lanes. Planners hope that more people will leave their cars at home.

Above In built up areas, there is always a lack of space for good transport networks. One solution is to build a flyover, which takes one road above another.

'Park and Ride' schemes encourage people to leave their cars outside the city in special car parks, where they can then hop on a bus into the centre. Cycle lanes also help cyclists to beat the traffic and choose pedal power!

If we change the way we get around, using public transport and pollution-free methods of transport, the environment of many inner cities will gradually improve.

Left In busy inner-city streets everyone needs help to get across the road! This school crossing patrol lady makes sure that people get across the road safely.

Activity

Sometimes, just getting to and from work or school can be a nightmare in an inner city. Design a board game to show your journey to school. It could look something like the game shown here.

You can follow the style of the example in this book, but try to include some funny things that might happen on your own journey to school. Think about all the different methods of transport which you and your friends use to get to school, and add these to your game.

When you have designed your game and coloured it in, all you will need is a die, some counters and some friends to play it with – have fun!

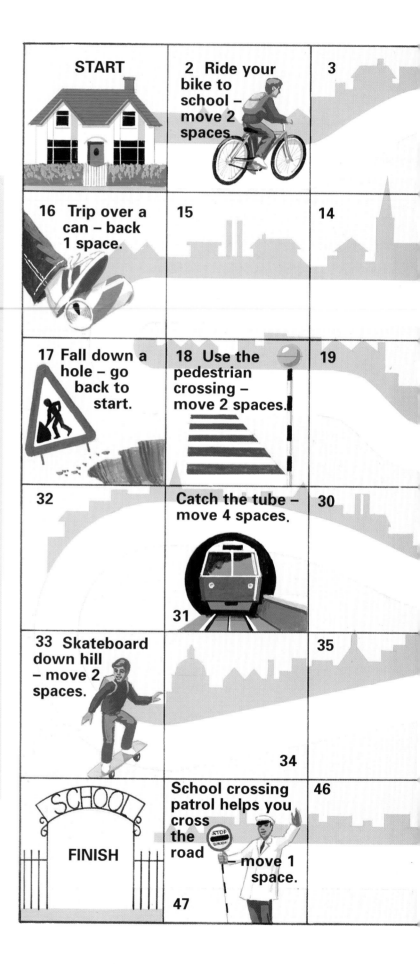

START

2 Ride your bike to school – move 2 spaces.

3

16 Trip over a can – back 1 space.

15

14

17 Fall down a hole – go back to start.

18 Use the pedestrian crossing – move 2 spaces.

19

32

Catch the tube – move 4 spaces.

30

31

33 Skateboard down hill – move 2 spaces.

35

34

FINISH

School crossing patrol helps you cross the road – move 1 space.

46

47

4	**5** Red traffic light – miss a turn.	**6 Chased by a dog –** back 2 spaces.	**7**	**8 Breathe in traffic fumes – back 1 space.**
13	**12 Traffic – miss a turn.**	**11**	**10 Catch the tram – move 1 space.**	**9**
20	**21**	**22 Driven by car – miss a turn.**	**23 Stop for sweets – miss a turn.**	**24**
29	**28** Traffic accident – back 2 spaces.	**27**	**26**	**25 Flat tyre – miss a turn.**
36	**37 Drop books – miss a turn.**	**38 Take a short cut – move 2 spaces.**	**39**	**40**
45	**44 The headmaster offers you a lift –** move 2 spaces.	**43**	**Your watch is fast – move 1 space.** **42**	**41**

Shopping and Entertainment

Colourful markets, parks, sports arenas, shops and cafés are all part of the inner city. There is more variety in shopping and entertainment than in any other kind of settlement. Many suburbs have large housing estates which were built without any shops at all. For most villages, the nearest shopping centre, cinema or swimming pool is several kilometres away. In an inner city, all these facilities are usually only a short walk or bus ride away.

Above The gateway to Manchester's Chinatown. People can buy special Chinese foods here that they cannot find in ordinary supermarkets.

Right Large football grounds are often located in inner cities. Every Saturday, thousands of people pour into cities such as Manchester, Leeds and Liverpool to watch their favourite football players.

Castlefield Urban Heritage Park

Castlefield, an inner-city area of Manchester, was once a thriving industrial area. It has now been transformed into the UK's first Urban Heritage Park. Thousands of people visit Castlefield every year.

The Power Hall at Castlefield.

Castlefield is located on the Bridgewater Canal, which was built in the eighteenth century for the Duke of Bridgewater. Barges brought coal from the Duke's mines in Worsley, helping to make Manchester a wealthy city. Today, Castlefield's old buildings have been redeveloped. The exciting Museum of Science and Industry can be found in the world's oldest railway station. There are also new buildings, such as the huge G-Mex Centre, which is used for pop concerts and exhibitions.

Inner cities have small local facilities, such as corner shops, local parks and libraries, as well as large department stores, restaurants and theatres in the city centre. There are also specialist shops, restaurants and markets selling the clothes and foods of different ethnic groups living in the area. In Leicester, there is a whole area of shops specializing in beautiful fabrics used for traditional Indian saris. In London, busy street markets in Notting Hill and Shepherds Bush have stalls selling West Indian fruit and vegetables.

A new lease of life

Over the last fifty years, there have been changes in shopping and entertainment in the inner-city areas. The decline in manufacturing industries has led to unemployment. Many people now have less money to spend. With fewer customers many small shops have closed down, and are left empty and derelict. In some areas, once-thriving shopping parades are now empty. People also worry about crime there.

Activity

Out of town shopping centres are not popular with everyone. Try acting out a debate with your friends between an out-of-town supermarket developer and a small local shopkeeper. Make a start by listing your arguments for and against.

Below Meadowhall Shopping Centre in Sheffield, is full of hundreds of shops all under one roof. Meadowhall has cinemas and restaurants too. So many services in one place attracts people away from smaller local shops.

The decline of inner-city shopping has been made worse by shops and businesses moving to out-of-town shopping centres, where land prices are cheaper than in inner cities and the road networks are better. Many shoppers now prefer to use these centres, because they can do all their shopping in one place. There is also plenty of space to park, and there are often cinemas and restaurants. Small shopkeepers find it hard to compete, and planners are now limiting such developments to stop more inner-city shops closing down.

Cities all over the UK are now trying to encourage people back into the inner cities to do their shopping and for entertainment. Pedestrian-only areas have been built to make shopping more enjoyable, and special security cameras help people feel safer, especially at night. As old industrial areas are redeveloped, the buildings are being turned into museums and theatres, and derelict land is used for parks, city farms, and even dry ski slopes!

Some inner city shopping areas such as this one in Liverpool have been made more attractive by planting trees.

37

Inner Cities and the Future

In all the major cities in the UK, planners are thinking of the future and are looking at all the exciting things that an inner city has to offer. Planners have begun projects to help solve some of the problems and to highlight the benefits of living in an inner city.

Empty industrial buildings, such as old factories and warehouses, which once brought wealth to the cities, are now being redeveloped for new businesses. Some businesses have moved to out-of-town business parks. But planners believe it is better for the environment to redevelop old, run-down areas, instead of using up new, unspoilt green areas. City grants are given for such redevelopments.

This was how planners saw the Olympic Stadium, in Manchester. This was part of Manchester's bid to host the year 2000 Olympics.

Some cities, such as Manchester and Cardiff, have also set up urban repdevelopment projects to advertise the many good things about inner-city life. The area of Hulme, in inner-city Manchester, was the site for the Olympic Stadium when the UK made a bid to host the year 2000 Olympics. Although Manchester did not win the bid, a great deal of money has been invested in this area. The newly built Metrolink tram has improved transport, and old, run-down houses have been knocked down and replaced with new ones.

The central square at Brindleyplace is a lively public space, enjoyed by visitors and local people.

Brindleyplace, Birmingham

Brindleyplace is described as the 'Birmingham of tomorrow', and shows how successful redevelopment of a run-down industrial area can be. Brindleyplace is named after James Brindley, the famous canal builder of the Industrial Revolution. It is a mixture of new offices, homes, restaurants, shops, an art gallery and a grand public square.

The heart of Brindleyplace is the Water's Edge area, which is built by the side of the canals which first made the city wealthy. There is also a magnificent, traffic-free public square, with gardens and a huge fountain. The People Place is especially popular with children, as it has the largest Sea Life Centre in England!

Brindleyplace has mixed modern building designs with old buildings. Oozells Street School, one of Birmingham's oldest schools, has been renovated, and is now a world-famous art gallery. Old cobble-stone pavements have also helped to give the development a 'feel for the past', in a very modern setting.

Planning for the future

For such changes to be successful, planners have learnt that they must ask people who live in inner cities what kinds of improvements they want. Most have said that there is a need for good quality housing for young, single people, as well as for families. Green spaces are also very important in densely populated areas, which are tightly packed with people, cars and buildings.

This is Canary Wharf, in the heart of London's new, redeveloped Docklands area.

In London, the inner-city Docklands area has been redeveloped, but not everyone is in favour of the way it has changed. Some of the local people, who have lived in the area for years, feel that too many luxury flats and offices were built and not enough lower-priced housing. Other changes have been more popular. In 1996, Belfast's beautiful Waterfront Hall opened for exhibitions and entertainment. This helped to create many new jobs in an area where unemployment was high, due to the decline in the shipbuilding industry.

Above **These inner-city high-rise flats are getting a face lift.**

In Leeds, the inner city used to be deserted at night due to fear of crime and having few places for entertainment. Now, Leeds is being transformed into the first twenty-four-hour city in the UK. Night-clubs are allowed to stay open late, and there are lots of street cafés, markets and fun fairs. The aim is that at any time of the day or night, the city will be alive with music, dancing and entertainment.

Inner cities are learning to cope with the changes they have faced, and planners are working hard to improve their future.

Above **This bustling street café in Leeds is a popular place for people to meet.**

41

How to Investigate an Inner City

There are many ways to start investigating an inner city. Below are some ideas for you to consider as a starting point for your research.

First-hand information

Local newspapers include interesting news items about daily life in an inner city. The letters page will especially show you what people think about proposed changes and future plans for the area. National newspapers, magazines and television programmes also have lots of features on inner-city life.

People in the know

Parents, teachers, relatives and neighbours are likely to have visited or lived in cities. Try talking to them about their experiences.

Your local library can provide all kinds of information about inner cities. The reference section is particularly useful. The librarian will help you to find census information, Ordnance Survey maps, books, encyclopaedias, magazines and newspapers.

The planning departments of city councils can send you information about future plans for the area, along with facts and figures. City councils may also have a special Education Officer, who can help you with this kind of research. To find out where to begin, try contacting the public relations office.

Maps

There are a variety of maps to look at when studying an inner city. A road atlas usually has city or town plans at the back, showing all the major cities in the UK. An A–Z-style street map will show you all the local roads, green areas, important buildings and stations. An Ordnance Survey map will give you all this in much more detail.

Census information

Census information shows us how particular areas have changed over the years, and what they are like now. The

information includes the numbers of people living in an area and their ages, whether or not they are single, married or divorced, where they were born, whether they are working, unemployed or retired, what kind of housing they live in and whether or not they own a car. You can find census information in a large public library.

Places to visit

Try to visit museums, urban study centres, visitor's centres sometimes found in large factories or businesses, tourist information offices, parks or city farms.

Collecting and presenting your evidence

Collect all the information you find, such as leaflets, bus or train tickets, museum guides, postcards and newspaper cuttings, and design your own inner-city scrap book or poster promoting the area. Think about using other types of media, such as CD-rom encyclopaedias, photographs or tape recordings of interviews. Also, if you have access to a computer, you could try entering your findings on a database.

Notes About this Book

The main text in each book in the Landmarks series provides general information about one of four types of settlements within the contexts of communities, work, schools, transport, shopping and entertainment, and change. Each book in the series features the same areas of study so that the four different types of settlements can be compared easily with each other within a general context.

Case studies give specific information about a particular aspect of each chapter and often provide direct quotes from people who live and work in different kinds of settlements. Children can use this information to make a direct comparison with their own experience.

The activities are designed so that children from any type of settlement can do them. The activities can be used to demonstrate what the main text has already stated about the locality mentioned in the book, or as a contrast. Throughout the series children are encouraged to work with the various tools that a geographer uses to study a particular area, such as mapping and graph skills, conducting surveys and using primary source evidence such as census material.

Introduction (pages 4–7)
This chapter gives a brief outline of what inner cities are and how they have developed. Children are encouraged to look around them, and either compare or contrast their own settlement with that of an inner city. The text examines what features make inner cities urban settlements, why some cities are situated in specific locations and how they differ from each other. You could find out what the children already know about inner cities and use this discussion to bring out examples from the text. Do the children have their own ideas about why inner cities are so densely populated or why they have grown up where they are?

Activity on page 7:
This activity encourages the children to analyse the structure of a city, using a basic model and a city plan. Using a plan with the main buildings marked children will be able to locate the central business district and the more built-up areas of the settlement. They should also be able to locate areas of dense housing and notice how the density of buildings decreases towards the outskirts of the settlement.

People and Communities (pages 8–13)
This chapter looks at the wide variety of communities in an inner city. Children are encouraged to examine how and why a community has changed. You might ask your children to gather information about where they live from adults living in the area. Encourage children to talk to someone who has lived in the community for many years about what the area used to be like. Discuss the types of housing found in inner cities and what advantages or disadvantages there may be.

Activity on page 11:
Census information provides useful clues about a settlement. In this activity, children are asked to examine some census information and see how it can be used by planners to decide how many schools may be needed in the future. Analyse census material for your area. What other information does it provide about the population? Compare it with previous years. Has the population risen or fallen?

Earning a Living (pages 14–19)
This chapter examines the different types of employment found in inner cities. You could ask your children to think about topics such as unemployment and the decline of industry. Is there any evidence of industry still visible in your locality? What kinds of jobs can they think of in the service industry?

Activity on page 19:
This activity encourages children to think about the types of jobs that family members and friends do. Can the different jobs be divided into groups such as services, manufacturing and industry? Can the children see any changing patterns of employment between the generations?

Inner City Schools (pages 20–25)
This chapter asks the children to think about their school environment. They are encouraged to compare or contrast their school and its surrounding neighbourhood with the inner city examples mentioned in the text. How many children are there in their classes? Are there any striking features about their school building? Do these features suggest any clues about the school's past?

Activity on page 24:
This simple mapping activity encourages children to think about their school and its surrounding area. What shops and services are nearby? Are there pedestrian crossings or bus stops? Are there any green spaces in the area?

On the Move (pages 26–33)
This chapter focuses on the importance of good communication networks, and the environmental implications of modern forms of transport. Discuss issues such as traffic congestion and pollution, and ask the children to suggest ways in which this might be reduced. In what ways might public transport be improved to encourage more people to use it?

Activity on page 32–3:
This is a fun way of getting children to think about the advantages or disadvantages of different methods of transport. You might encourage them to touch on as many issues as possible such as congestion, pollution and road safety.

Shopping and Entertainment (pages 34– 37)
This chapter examines the changing nature of shopping and entertainment in inner cities. Discuss with the children what types of facilities exist in your locality. Do people choose to shop in the large department stores and supermarkets, or do they prefer to shop in smaller, specialist shops? Why?

Activity on page 36:
This activity is designed to promote a debate. With a group of children, discuss the various issues involved first, elect a chairperson and about three children to argue each case. The rest of the group can then vote for or against and ask questions from the floor.

Change and the Future: (pages 38–41)
This chapter encourages children to think about the changing face of inner cities. Discuss some of the problems faced by people living in inner cities and what can be done to make them more attractive places to live. Touch on issues such as crime, pollution and homelessness.

Glossary

Artificial When something is not natural, but has been made by people.

Commuted Travelled to work.

Congested When a road has become blocked up.

Declined When something has become worse.

Estuary The part of a river that runs into the sea.

Exported Goods which are sent out of one country to be sold in another.

Facilities Places that provide services.

Imported Brought in to be sold in the UK.

Industrial Revolution The time during the eighteenth and early nineteenth century when the development of new machinery led to the growth of factories in the UK.

Manufacturing Making things in a factory, using machines.

Networks Patterns of roads that fit together so that people can move from one place to another.

Planners People who make plans about the development of an area, usually working for the city council.

Raw materials Natural products such as coal, iron ore or wood.

Refugees People who move from one country to another to escape danger, such as war or cruelty.

Renovated Repaired and improved.

Royal Charter Permission given by a king or queen to use the title of 'city'.

Settlement A place where people live.

Transformed When something has changed completely.

Urban The name given to a built-up settlement with more than 5,000 people.

Victorian During the time of the reign of Queen Victoria (1837–1901).

Books To Read

Global Cities by Philip Parker (Wayland, 1994)
Where I Live – Inner City by Neil Thomsom (Watts Books, 1994)
Settlements by David Flint (Heinemann, 1993)
Settlements by Nick Millea (Wayland, 1992)
Town Life by Philip Parker (Wayland, 1994)
United Kingdom by Peter Evans (BBC Educational Publishing, 1996)

This map shows the cities which are mentioned in this book.

N

Glasgow

Newcastle

Belfast

Bradford Leeds
Manchester
Liverpool Sheffield
Nottingham
Birmingham Leicester
Coventry

Cardiff
Bristol London

0   50   100   150   200 km
0   50   100 miles

Index